Unicorn Affirmations

Dedicated to:
My 7 G-Babies

Published by

INK Bubbles PUBLISHING

Port Elgin, Ontario,

Canada

2021

Copyright © 2021 by Jewel Star

All rights reserved. This book or any portion thereof

may not be reproduced or used in any manner whatsoever.

without the express written permission of the Author/Publisher

except for the use of brief quotations in a book review.

ISBN   978-1-7770829-5-6

Unicorn Affirmations

Created By Jewel Star

I am... a good friend

I am... strong

I am... helpful

I am... smart

I am... amazing

I am...
kind

I am... loved

I am...
fun

I am...
happy

I am...
awesome

I am... important

I am... proud of myself

I am... special

I am... creative

I am...
patient

I am...
brave

I am... enough

I
love
me

Thank you for purchasing this book.

Follow Me on Instagram @Jewel Star Writer

Look for my other Children's Picture Books,

YA Books, Planners, Journals, Cookbooks,

Coloring Books, and other

genres.

Published by INK Bubbles Publishing

2021

www.ingramcontent.com/pod-product-compliance
Lightning Source LLC
Chambersburg PA
CBHW042144030726
47599CB00002B/606